THE HERMITAGE

A Tour of the Halls and Rooms

Foreword by
Mikhail Piotrovsky

Texts by
Sophia Kudriavtseva and Liudmila Torshina

Editor-in-Chief
Nina Grishina

Edited by
Maria Lyzhenkova

Translated from the Russian by
Paul Williams (Foreword) and Valery Fateyev (Texts)

Designed by Vitaly Viazovsky

Photographs by
Pavel Demidov, Leonard Kheifets, Romuald Kirillov,
Vladimir Mikhailov, Yuri Molodkovets, Victor Savik,
Yevgeny Siniaver, Georgy Skachkov, Vladimir Terebenin
and Oleg Trubsky

Computer type-setting by
Olga Dubovaya

Colour correction by
Yekaterina Shumikhina

Colour-separated films produced by Goland Company,
St Petersburg

ISBN 5-94795-058-8

The Hermitage is not only a repository of masterpieces of world art, but also a great monument of Russian culture, a symbol of its openness to the world and involvement with world culture as a whole. This fundamental world-wide quality comprises one of the unique features of the Hermitage. The museum has a non-Russian name — "Hermitage", from the French meaning "a hermit's dwelling" or "a place of solitude". It was fashionable in the eighteenth century to give the name to cosy palatial pavilions adjoining the palaces of monarchs where the exalted host or hostess could entertain a narrow circle of selected guests without concern for the strict rules of courtly etiquette. Times have changed, but still today the museum remains for sensitive people and those who love art "a place of solitude" where art allows a person to enter a one-to-one relationship with world culture, to immerse him or herself in the world of eternal thoughts and feelings, the world of beauty and poetry. This is the great mission of the Hermitage at the start of the twenty-first century.

The great museum has a host of faces, changing from building to building and from era to era. The Winter Palace is a masterpiece of the Russian Baroque. Now its state rooms house displays of French art, silver and porcelain. Yet the spirit of the reigns of its former occupants lives on in it — Catherine the Great, Alexander I, the age of Nicholas I and the time of the Tsar-Liberator Alexander II. The former rooms for ladies-in-waiting now contain the paintings of Matisse and Picasso, Chinese frescoes and the silver vessels of Sasanian shahanshahs. The Small Hermitage is the dwelling-place of the "Semiramis of the North" as Voltaire dubbed Catherine the Great, the creator of the Hermitage. On display here today is an extremely rich collection of mediaeval art: the Bazilewsky Collection, rare works by old Netherlandish painters. The Old, or Large, Hermitage was created specially for Catherine's growing collections. Today it contains the paintings of Leonardo, Titian and masters of the Italian Renaissance. The Hermitage Theatre is today, as in Catherine's time, the venue for operas and ballets, while beneath its stage the Winter Palace of Peter the Great has been excavated and reconstructed. The New Hermitage, whose entrance is flanked by Terebenev's mighty atlantes, is one of the world's finest examples of museum architecture. Masterpieces of ancient sculpture, the canvases of Veronese and Tiepolo, of Dutch and Flemish masters, as well as elaborate knightly arms and armour are all like precious stones mounted in the classical setting of Russia's first public museum. The east wing of the General Staff building is also now part of the Hermitage. The rooms of tsarist ministries planned by Rossi are gradually turning into museum halls. The Hermitage has come to embody the great history of Russia. It preserves the spirit and images of its great rulers and heroes. It presents the whole of world culture in some of its most exalted masterpieces. To take a trip through the halls of the Hermitage means to travel the whole world.

Mikhail Piotrovsky,
Director of the State Hermitage,
Corresponding Member of the Russian Academy of Sciences,
Full Member of the Russian Academy of Arts,
Professor of St Petersburg University,
Doctor of Historical Sciences

Louis Tocqué. 1696– 1772
Portrait of Empress Elizabeth Petrovna. *1758. Oil on canvas*

View of the Winter Palace by Night. *1857*
Watercolour by Vasily Sadovnikov

The Hermitage, a world-famous museum, the pride of Russia, is a complex of beautiful buildings running along the Neva in the centre of St Petersburg. The five palaces located between the Neva and Palace Square, as well as the wing of the General Staff building enclosing the square from the south, the Menshikov Palace on the opposite side of the river and the stock repository in Novaya Derevnia, house immense treasures. Nearly three million exhibits — more than 16,000 paintings, 12,000 pieces of sculpture, about 600,000 works of graphic art, over 250,000 objects of applied art, 700,000 archaeological finds, 1,000,000 numismatic items and rich collections of books — represent the culture and art of the peoples of the world from the Palaeolithic to the twentieth century.

The Hermitage exists for 240 years. The date of its foundation is taken to be 1764, the year of acquisition of the first group of paintings. However, the history of the Hermitage had begun earlier, with the construction of its first edifice, the Winter Palace. The main residence of the Russian Emperors, the Winter Palace was erected in 1754—61 by the architect Francesco

Bartolomeo Rastrelli for Empress Elizabeth Petrovna. Its first owner, however, became Catherine the Great. It was she who conceived the idea to create, according to a French fashion, a *hermitage* within the royal palace, for receptions and entertainment in a narrow circle of guests. Thus the present-day Small Hermitage — the Hanging Gardens with the South and North Pavilions linked by galleries — emerged to the east of the Winter Palace in 1764—75. It was there that Catherine's first acquisitions were accommodated. The Empress started in 1764 with 225 paintings acquired from the Berlin merchant Johann Gotzkowsky and towards the end of her reign she

Franz Krüger. 1797—1857
Portrait of Emperor Nicholas I
Oil on canvas. 1850s

The New Hermitage. *1861*
Watercolour by Luigi Premazzi

owned one of the best collections in Europe. In 1771–87, to house the growing collections, one more building, the Old Hermitage, was added. And in 1783–87 the complex of Catherine's Hermitage palaces was enlarged by Giacomo Quarenghi with the newly built Raphael Loggias and the Hermitage Theatre.

The heirs of Catherine the Great increased the riches of the Hermitage and turned it from a private collection into the Imperial Public Museum. Nicholas I played the principal role in its creation. Between 1839 and 1851 a special museum building, the New Hermitage, that completed the ensemble of the Hermitage palaces, was put up on his orders. An impressive portico with the figures of granite atlantes on the side of Millionnaya Street served as an entrance to the museum. Until the revolution of 1917 the museum was the imperial family's property and a part of the royal residence. The fall of monarchy in March 1917 and the taking of the palace by mutinous sailors, workers and soldiers in October 1917 became a boundary, after which a new history of the museum began. Its collections augmented four times; new departments were opened and the museum's science widened the scope of its activities. The Hermitage

The Room of Dutch and Flemish Schools in the New Hermitage (The Tent-Roof Hall). *1858*
Watercolour by Luigi Premazzi

7

The throne speech of Emperor Nicholas II before the opening of the First State Duma in the St George Hall of the Winter Palace. Photograph. 1906

Unknown artist. Portrait of Emperor Nicholas II. *1915– 16. Oil on canvas*

Mikhail Rundaltsev. Portriat of Empress Alexandra Fiodorovna. *1905. Oil on canvas*

Pavel Sokolov-Skalia. 1899—1961
The Assault of the Winter Palace. 1957. *Oil on canvas*

had a troublesome period in the 1930s when a number of its famous masterpieces were sold abroad. The museum courageously lived through the severe years of the Second World War and the siege of Leningrad. The end of the twentieth century became for the Hermitage a time of renovation and new acquisitions. The old building of the Menshikov Palace was made a branch of the Hermitage; in 1987—89 the Hermitage Theatre had a major restoration and on its ground floor were reconstructed several rooms of the early Winter Palace put up for Peter the Great. At the beginning of the 1990s the left wing of the General Staff Building was given to the Hermitage Museum and the former Tsar's ministries were used to arrange new exhibitions. In the summer of 2003 the cast-iron gates of the three-arched entrance to the Winter Palace on the side of Palace Square have been flung open for visitors to the Winter Palace, inviting thousands of guests to make an exciting tour of the museum's halls and rooms.

> View of the Winter Palace from the Neva

The Main (Jordan) Staircase. 1754—62; 1837—39
Architects: Francesco Bartolomeo Rastrelli; Vasily Srasov

A tour of the Hermitage interiors begins from the noisy vestibule with its ticket offices, cloak rooms and Information Service. On passing through a vast gallery, we enter the shaded vaults of the staircase flight, go up several stairs — and suddenly an immense space unfolds before our eyes: Olympic gods are soaring at an inaccessible height; light is pouring from the windows, reflected in mirrors and is sliding along the white walls, pilasters and statues; the gold of moulded ornaments is shimmering. The two wide flights of the white marble staircase lead us upwards. Ten granite columns rise majestically over the landing of the first floor making us raise our eyes, look around and enjoy the majesty of the Baroque decor of the Main Staircase. This sumptuous entrance amazed the first visitors to the palace, the guests of Empress Catherine the Great. The staircase has almost completely retained the appearance created by Rastrelli.

The Main (Jordan) Staircase. Upper landing

The Large Field Marshal Hall. *1866*
Watercolour by Eduard Hau

The entrance from the Main Staircase of the palace leads to the Large Suite of sumptuous rooms. It opens with the Field Marshal Hall: once portraits of Russian Field Marshals decorated this interior. Officers stood on guard in this room and visitors could watch a majestic ceremony of guard mounting and relieving. The austere architecture in the style of Classicism, the motifs of painted and moulded decor and the bronze chandeliers made up of trophies — the depictions of arms and armour — as well as the portraits of Russian Field Marshals that had once decorated the walls and gave their name to the hall — all serves to commemorate the military glory of Russia. The interior was created together with the neighbouring Peter Hall by the architect Auguste de Montferrand in 1833—34. But a fire that broke out in December 1837 destroyed the decor of the halls and rooms. In 1838—39 they were re-created closely to the original concept by Vasily Stasov, who supervised the work on the restoration of the palace. Today this interior is an introductory hall to the exhibitions of the Hermitage.

The large coronation carriage. 1720s. Paris, France
Carved wood, cast and gilded metal, glass,
leather, silk, cloth; embroidery, painting. Length 700 cm
Acquired by Peter the Great in Paris in 1717; probably used
during the coronation of Catherine the Great in 1763

Jacopo Amiconi. 1675–1752. **Peter the Great with the Goddess of Wisdom Minerva.** *Detail Between 1732 and 1735. Oil on canvas. 231 x 178 cm*

The Peter Hall was created in honour of Emperor Peter the Great, the founder of the Russian Empire. On the white Lyons velvet lining the walls are embroidered the coats of arms and monograms of Peter the Great repeated at the bases of the walls and in the ceiling painting. Above are the paintings depicting Peter's victories in the war against Sweden — *The Battle of Poltava* and *The Battle of Lesnaya*. In the semicircular niche, like in the chancel of an Orthodox church, framed by jasper columns, is a painting representing the Emperor with Minerva, the goddess of wisdom and war. In front of the painting is the throne of Emperor Paul I executed by the master Ch. Mayer in 1797.

The Peter Hall (Small Throne Room) 1833; 1838–39 Architects: Auguste de Montferrand; Vasily Stasov

The Armorial Hall. Detail

Behind the Peter Hall there unfolds the space of the Armorial Hall, one of the largest interiors in the Winter Palace, about 1000 square metres in area. The slender Corinthian colonnade supporting the choir, the sculptural groups of Russian warriors at the sides of the entrances, lend to the hall an air of festive solemnity. It was here that the Emperor received representatives of the provincial gentry and Russian cities: mounted on the chandeliers are shields with coats of arms of the Russian provinces. The Armorial Hall houses an exhibition of Western European silver of the seventeenth and eighteenth centuries. The festive tableware and vessels — services, table decorations or *plats de ménages*, wine-coolers — all commissioned by the Russian Court and the nobility from the well-known craftsmen of Paris and Augsburg, neighbour elegant knick-knacks and pieces of jewellery here.

The Armorial Hall. 1838—39. Architect: Vasily Stasov

The Armorial Hall adjoins the 1812 War Gallery — an architectural and pictorial monument to the feat of the Russian warriors, who gained a victory over the armies of the French Emperor Napoleon Bonaparte. The gallery was built by the architect Carlo Rossi and opened in 1826. On its walls hang 332 portraits of Russian generals — participants in the campaigns of 1812—15: The portraits were produced in 1819—28 by the English painter George Dawe, mostly from

George Daw. 1781— 1829. Portrait of Prince Piotr Bagration. Ca 1823. Oil on canvas. 70 x 62.5 cm

George Daw. 1781— 1829
Portrait of Prince Nikolai Rayevsky
Ca 1825. Oil on canvas. 70 x 62.5 cm

George Daw. 1781— 1829
Portrait of Prince Mikhail Kutuzov. 1829
Oil on canvas. 361 x 268 cm

The Gallery of 1812

life; portraits of killed warriors were done from life-time representations. Thirteen frames, however, were left blank — that was the way chosen to commemorate those warriors whose portraits had not been found. During the great fire that raged in the palace in 1837 the soldiers of the palatial Grenadiers Company, veterans of the War of 1812, saved the portraits. The gallery was restored to its original appearance. On the butt-end wall, under a canopy, is set a portrait of Emperor Alexander I by Franz Krüger. The most honourable place in front of the entrance to the main, Large Throne Hall, is occupied by portraits of Mikhail Barclay de Tolly, the Commander-in-Chief of the Russian Army, and Mikhail Kutuzov, who defeated Napoleon.

The Large Throne Room (the St George Hall). 1838—41
Architect: Vasily Stasov

The suite of state rooms ends with the Large Throne Room. Here, on a platform covered with velvet, against the background of the state emblem of the Russian Empire, is set the throne executed for Empress Anna Ioannovna in 1737 by the English craftsman Nicholas Clausen. This room was the venue for the principal ceremonies of the imperial court, and the days of St George and St Catherine are celebrated today as official "days of the Hermitage". The hall was created on the place of the Throne Room of Catherine the Great built by Giacomo Quarenghi. Having retained the former plan, Stasov designed the hall in the style of Classicism facing it with white Carrara marble and ormolu. Sumptuous parquet floor of sixteen kinds of wood echoes the gilded ornaments of the ceiling.

The Large Throne Room. The Throne place

The Large Church adjoins the Large Suite of state rooms. It was used for religious services which were an indispensable part of official ceremonies, festive services for the royal families and the court, weddings and baptism. The church preserves its sumptuous Baroque appearance created by Rastrelli and revived by Stasov after the fire of 1837. The church interior serves as a fine setting for exhibitions of Christian art held here.

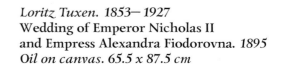

Loritz Tuxen. 1853— 1927
**Wedding of Emperor Nicholas II
and Empress Alexandra Fiodorovna.** *1895*
Oil on canvas. 65.5 x 87.5 cm

The Large Church of the Winter Palace. 1754—62; 1838—39
Architects: Bartolomeo Francesco Rastrelli; Vasily Stasov

The Exhibition of 18th-Century French Art
(The Drawing Room of the First Reserve Section)
1837—39. Architect: Alexander Briullov

We pass from the Large Church to the rooms of the first floor running along Palace Square. In the eighteenth century these rooms belonged to Catherine the Great (Rooms 272—281) and to her son, the future Emperor Paul I (Rooms 283—297). Newly designed by the architect Alexander Briullov after a fire of 1837, they became reserve apartments. Especially sumptuous are the drawing-rooms overlooking the square (Rooms 343—349), in whose design the theme of Russia's military glory is reflected: before the Revolution of 1917 it was used for displaying battle paintings and their vaults have retained to this day painted decor with military attributes. After the Winter Palace became a part of the Hermitage Museum in 1922, these interiors were converted into display rooms — now they accommodate the exhibition of French art of the fifteenth to eighteenth century.

André Charles Boulle. 1642—1732
Cupboard. 2nd half of the 17th century. Paris
Ebony, ormolu, marquetry. 255 x 170 x 64 cm

Almost all French artists active in the course of three and a half centuries are represented in the twenty-five rooms of this display. Paintings, sculpture, "items of luxury", for which France was famous — furniture, tapestries, fabrics and embroideries, porcelain, etc. — this is one of the best collection of French art all over the world. The nucleus of the collection was formed in the eighteenth century thanks to numerous purchases and commissions made for the founder of the Hermitage, Empress Catherine the Great. The collection was replenished later, too, especially after 1917, when objects of art from nationalized private collections were transferred to the Hermitage. Especially well represented in the Hermitage collection is the classical or "grand" period of French art — the seventeenth century.

Service with cameos. 1778—79. Sèvres, Paris
Software, commissioned by Catherine the Great
It contains more than 700 pieces.

Nicolas Poussin. 1594—1665
Tancred and Erminia. 1630—31. *Oil on canvas. 98.5 x 146.5 cm*

Depictions of peasants against the background of northern France look like an embodiment of wisdom and dignity in the masterpiece of Louis Le Nain, known as the "painter of reality" — he represented a realist trend in art of the early seventeenth century. Twelve pictures acquaint visitors with the work of Nicolas Poussin, a leader of the French school of painting. A creator of the national style of Classicism, he sought to express lofty ideals drawing on examples of Classical Antiquity and the Renaissance. The theme of love acquired a lofty overtone in Poussin's famous painting *Tancred and Erminia*, a pride of the Hermitage collection. A subtle lyricism and a sense of elegant beauty of colour permeate the world of ideal nature in the landscapes of Claude Lorrain — a major master of Classicism, whose works occupy a whole separate room in the museum.

Louis Le Nain. 1593—1648
The Milkwoman's Family. *1640s. Oil on canvas. 51 x 59 cm*

Antoine Watteau. 1684– 1721
Capricious Girl. Ca 1718. Oil on canvas. 42 x 34 cm

On leaving the rooms of serious and elevated art of the seventeenth century, we find ourselves in the varied world of French eighteenth-century art. The "gallant age", the century of free thinking and the Enlightenment" was the period of the emergence of new ideals permeated with a presentiment of a forthcoming revolution. At the beginning of the century stands the figure of a solitary dreamer Antoine Watteau, who implemented subtle intimate feelings in colours for the first time.

François Boucher. 1703— 1770
Pastoral Scene. 1740s. Oil on canvas. 61 x 75 cm

Jean Honoré Fragonard. 1732— 1806. **The Snatched Kiss**
Late 1780s. Oil on canvas. 45 x 55 cm

Jean-Baptiste Siméon Chardin. 1699—1779. **Still Life with the Attributes of the Arts.** *1766. Oil on canvas. 112 x 140.5 cm*

His elegant and ironic *scènes galantes* are veritable masterpieces. Watteau's influence made itself felt on the formation of the Rococo style predominant in eighteenth-century art. Works by its leading master, Boucher, are represented in a wide stylistic context, side by side with Falconet's marble pieces, Fragonard's paintings, furniture and precious objects. In opposition to the Rococo stands Chardin's serious art maintaining the beauty of simple and eternal ideas. Chardin's *Still Life* and his masterpieces *The Washerwoman* and *Grace before Meat* neighbour sculptural pieces by Jean Antoine Houdon, who was active on the eve of the French Revolution and created images of famous figures of the Frenh Enlightenment.

Jean-Antoine Houdon. 1741— 1828
Voltaire in an Armchair. *1781. Marble. Height 138 cm*

The collection of German art of the fifteenth to eighteenth century runs parallel to the display of seventeenth-century French art, in the suite located above the courtyard, where in the age of Catherine the Great were the rooms of her State Secretaries. The collection is distinguished primarily by its masterpieces of the German Renaissance. The portrait of a young man full of dignity and harmony demonstrates the mastery of execution characteristic of the Holbein family of artists. The artist who painted this portrait, Ambrosius Holbein, was the son of Hans Holbein the Elder and the brother of Hans Hobein the Younger. Lucas Cranach the Elder, one of the leading masters of the Renaissance, is represented in the collection by four splendid paintings. Canopied by heavy

Lucas Cranach the Elder. 1472– 1553. **The Virgin under the Apple.** *Ca 1530. Oil on canvas. 87 x 59 cm*

fruits, his *Virgin under the Apple Tree* charms us by the femininity and mystery of her glance. The painting *Venus and Cupid* is the first ever depiction of a naked body in German art. Cranach endows the slender goddess with a somewhat threatening appearance and the Latin inscription over her head warns us: "Study with all your might to resist the voluptuous Cupid/Lest blind Love master your captive heart." The exhibition allows one to trace the history of the development of German art until Neo-Classicism in the late eighteenth century that is represented by works of Raphael Mengs, the most well-known master of this trend.

Ambrosius Holbein. Ca 1495 — ca 1520 **Portrait of a Young Man. 1518** *Oil and tempera on panel. 44 x 32.5 cm*

Joshua Reynolds. 1723— 1792
Cupid Untying the Zone of Venus. 1788
Oil on canvas. 127.5 x 101 cm

Next to the French exhibition, in the five rooms of one of the former reserve sections of the palace, overlooking the courtyard, is the exhibition of English art of the sixteenth to nineteenth century. English painting is represented here by varied and magnificent works, especially portraits, for which England was famous. One can also see here rare works of the English Renaissance, a long row of eighteenth-century portraits by Romney, Raeburn and Hoppner, and the pride of the Hermitage, Gainsborough's masterpiece — *Portrait of a Lady in Blue*. The flowering of English art is associated primarily with the work of Reynolds, the first President of the Royal Academy of Arts in London. The Hermitage owns three of his paintings. Especially famous are the canvas *The Infant Hercules Strangling the Serpents* — an allegory symbolizing Russia and executed as a commission of Catherine the Great, as well as the lyrical and sensual composition *Cupid Untying the Girdle of Venus*. There is an opinion that the artist's sitter for this painting was the famous beauty Lady Hamilton, a lover of Admiral Nelson.

Thomas Gainsborough. 1727—1788
Portrait of a Lady in Blue. *Late 1770s. Oil on canvas. 76 x 64 cm*

Hubert Robert. 1733—1808. **Landscape with a Ruin.** *Oil on canvas. 311 x 147 cm*

After the displays of France and England, in the south-western part of the Winter Palace, the majestic White Hall introduces us into the suite of living apartments of Empress Maria Alexandrovna (1824—80), Alexander II's wife. Created in 1838 by the architect Alexander Briullov and later partly renovated, they retained the appearance from the middle of the nineteenth century and are a magnificent monument of the palace's dwelling architecture. They serve as exhibition rooms today. The sumptuous White Hall, richly decorated by sculpture, displays French art of the late eighteenth century, in particular paintings by the artists who were active in Russia — Voille and Vigée-Le Brun, a portrait painter at the French and Russian courts. Especially impressive are Robert's large landscapes with Roman ruins. Furniture manufactured by David Roentgen, a famous German cabinet-maker of the eighteenth century, can also be seen here. The massive bureaus of elaborate architecture are provided with music-stands, secret drawers and sly mechanisms, including musical ones. Next to the Gold Room is the interior with the walls gilded all over and adorned with fireplaces of white marble and coloured mosaics. We can see here in showcases on the tables a rich collection of Western European engraved gems and semi-precious stones.

The White Hall. 1838—41
Architect: Alexander Briullov

Giovanni Pichler. 1734– 1791. Italy
Centaur and Bacchante. Second half
of the 18th century. Sardonyx. 1.7 x 2.4 cm

Portrait of Henri IV. 1596. France
Mother-of-pearl. 2.2 x 1.7 cm
Henri IV was the King of France
from 1594 to 1610

William Brown. 1748– 1825. England. The Head of
Hygea. 1785. Cornelian, in a gold mount. 3 x 2.7 cm
Hygea was an ancient Greek goddess of health,
daughter of Aesculapius, the god of healing

The Golden Drawing-Room. 1860s
Architect: Alexander Briullov

The Crimson Reception Room (Study). Late 1850s
Architect: Andrei Stakenschneider

After the state rooms of the living half of the building we reach more intimate private apartments. Next to the Golden Drawing-Room is a cosy interior of the family's Dining-Room with the walls of tender light-green shades. It was designed in the style of the French Rococo by the architect Andrei Stakenschneider. The moulded ornaments, paintings and mirrors create an elegant and sumptuous impression. Stakenschnei-der was also responsible for the design of the Empress's Crimson Room that replaced the Study created by Briull-ov. The walls of the Dining-Room are lined with damask executed from authentic nineteenth-century examples embroidered with depictions of music and musical instruments: the Drawing-Room was intended for musical parties. Now it is used to demonstrate examples of early English china — a part of the large collection of the Hermitage's Western European porcelain.

The Boudoir. 1853. Architect: Harald Bosse

From the elegant Crimson Room we are passing to the small, ornate, like a precious casket, Boudoir of the Empress. It is designed in the Rococo style — the red damask on the walls, the light network of gilded frames and ornaments, pictorial overdoor decorations... Seen in the depth of the interior is a cosy alcove on a small elevation under a wavy frame with caryatids. The furniture of French work was produced for the Boudoir in the same style and upholstered with the same brocade. The life-asserting luxury of the Boudoir contrasts with classically solemn, somewhat dark decor of the Blue Bedroom completing the enfilade. Nowadays it serves for mounting jewellery exhibitions. On leaving the apartments of Maria Alexandrovna, we raise to the second floor of the Winter Palace, to one of the most exciting exhibitions of the Hermitage — French art of the nineteenth and twentieth centuries.

The Blue Bedroom. 1838—41. Architect: Alexander Briullov

The exhibition of French art of the nineteenth and early twentieth centuries occupies twenty-five rooms on the second floor of the Winter Palace. This is one of the largest collections in the world, which reflects all the complexity of art life in France in that period. The first rooms introduce us to the atmosphere of the age that begun with the French Revolution and Napoleon's battles. It was in the crucible of these battles that new art was growing. Its recognized leader at the beginning of the nineteenth century was David — the first artist of the revolution and the Empire, the creator of the Neo-Classical school. Following the ideals of Classical An-

Antoine Jean Gros. 1771—1835
Napoleon Bonaparte on the Arcole Bridge. 1797
Oil on canvas. 134 x 104 cm

Jacques-Louis David. 1748— 1825
Sappho and Phaon. 1809. Oil on canvas. 225.3 x 262 cm

tiquity, David and his pupils asserted in art civic values and lofty deeds. Even the theme of love has a pathetic overtone in David's only Hermitage painting — the love of the poetess Sappho and Phaon is a source of Poetry! Gros depicted the young general Napoleon Bonaparte as an inspired hero calling his soldiers to follow him to a battle. In Gérard's portrait, Joséphine, Napoleon's wife, shown against a background of their palace at Malmaison, is beautiful like an ancient statue that came to life. In the age of the Empire Neo-Classicism became a general fashion, an "Imperial" style. It is present in the allegories by Prud'hon and Guérin and in everyday scenes by Boilly. But towards the end of the 1810s the cold grandeur of the

François Gérard. 1770— 1837
Portrait of Joséphine. 1801. Oil on canvas. 178 x 174 cm

Louis Léopold Boilly. 1761– 1845
Billiards. *1807. Oil on canvas. 56 x 81 cm*

Empire style and academic art met with opposition of the Romantic generation that was eager to attain more freedom in the expression of living human passions. The art of Romanticism is represented in the Hermitage by two masterpieces of the great Delacroix inspired by the East, Moroccan impressions and numerous works of less well-known artists. The discoveries of the Romanticists were getting fashionable, their themes and colouristic devices were skillfully reinterpreted by artists of the academic salons. Effective, but remote from life, salon art is represented in the display by paintings of the "admirable" Gérôme and portraits of Winterhalter, which illustrate the setting in which an innovative movement in art was under way. Realist artists made a decisive step in this direction towards

Jean-Léon Gérôme. 1824– 1904
The Sale of a Slave. *1884. Oil on canvas. 92 x 74 cm*

Eugène Delacroix. 1798—1863
Moroccan Saddling His Horse. 1855
Oil on canvas. 56 x 47 cm

Constantine Troyon. 1810–1865
On the Way to the Market. 1859
Oil on canvas. 260.5 x 211 cm

the middle of the nineteenth century. Proclaiming the principles of bringing art closer to life, the landscapists began to paint their canvases directly from life out-of-doors, working in the environs of the village of Barbizon near Paris. The whole section of the exhibition featuring works by Théodore Rousseau, the leader of the Barbizon school, and his adherents — Dupré, de la Peña, Troyon and Corot — leads us to the realm of quests which gave birth to the trend that changed the entire European art scene and is known as "Impressionism".

Théodore Rousseau. 1812–1867
Market in Normandy. 1832(?). Oil on canvas. 29.5 x 38 cm

Claude Oscar Monet. 1840– 1926. Lady in the Garden
(Sainte-Adresse). *1867. Oil on canvas. 80 x 99 cm*

Claude Oscar Monet. 1840—1926
A Corner of the Garden at Montgeron. 1876—77
Oil on canvas. 172 x 193 cm

We are entering the room of Claude Monet and it seems that the windows in front of us are widely open to the brightly illuminated world: the wind is swaying the flowers and ripples the water; the shady pond evokes a sense of coolness; the lady in a white dress is sliding with light steps over the grass; a bridge dissolves in a hazy London mist... This vibrant sense of living, translated into the idiom of painting, is a result of the creative method developed in the 1870s by Claude Monet and his friends Renoir, Sisley and Pissarro. After the first exhibition of paintings by these artists in Paris in 1874 they were nicknamed "Impressionists" (from the French word

Claude Oscar Monet. 1840— 1926. **The Pond at Montgeron.** *1876—77. Oil on canvas. 173 x 193 cm*

L'Impression as one of Monet's landscapes was entitled). This derisive name, however, was gradually accepted and began to be used for the method of painting in the open, under the impact of natural light and air medium. The Impressionist truly "captures" a fleeting moment of ever changing life. Thus the brush of Auguste Renoir arrested for a brief moment the movement of a boy — his figure seems to be woven of sun reflections and shades sliding along a sandy path and a green garden. In paintings by Camille Pissarro, the Paris of his time is represented as a casual glimpse of life in a large city. Even Edgar Degas, an artist who ignored plein-air — he painted his works in a studio — captures movements and gestures of his nudes

Edgar Degas. 1834– 1917. **Women Combing Her Hair (At the Toilet).** *1885. Pastel on cardboard. 53 x 52 cm*

Pierre Auguste Renoir. 1841– 1919
Child with a Whip. *1885. Oil on canvas. 105 x 75 cm*

Camille Pissarro. 1830–1903
Boulevard Montmartre in Paris. 1897. *Oil on canvas. 73 x 92 cm*

as if the women were surprised in their usual activities. Impressionism was the major phenomenon of French artistic life in the 1860s and 1870s. The altered European art scene is represented in the Hermitage by works of its leading masters — eight paintings by Monet, six superb works by Renoir, pictures by Sisley and Pissarro, as well as canvases by less well-known Impressionists. This collection, amassed at the turn of the nineteenth and twentieth centuries by Sergei Shchukin and Ivan Morozov, Moscow connoisseurs of the new painting, was transferred to the Hermitage in 1948. Now the Hermitage boasts one of the world's best collections of French art from the second half of the nineteenth and early twentieth centuries.

Paul Cézanne. 1839— 1906
The Smoker. *Ca 1890— 92. Oil on canvas. 92.5 x 73.5 cm*

From the paintings by the Impressionists we pass to the works of Post-Impressionist masters — artists active in the period at the turn of the nineteenth and twentieth centuries, after the last Impressionist exhibition held in 1886. Impressionism as a single movement ceased to exist, but it became a foundation, upon which began to take shape the art of "great individuals"— the misunderstood and rejected artists who opened up new paths in painting for the world. Eleven works by Cezanne from his early painting *Girl at the Piano* (1869), still naive in its thirst for independence, to his mastery of Impressionism in the 1870s and eventually to his world-

Vincent van Gogh. 1853—1890
The Lilac Bush. *1889. Oil on canvas. 72 x 92 cm*

Paul Gauguin. 1848–1903
Pastorales Tahitiennes. *1893. Oil on canvas. 87.5 x 113.7 cm*

famous masterpieces of the 1880s and 1890s, which have imbibed the heat of the southern sun and the cold grandeur of the mountains of Provence, the artist's homeland. The four paintings by Van Gogh painted at Arles and Auvers, in the period of the full flowering of his talent, bring to us his passionate, tragic feeling of life expressed in a riot of colours. The fifteen paintings by Gauguin created in Oceania, on the Tahiti and St Dominique islands, charm us by the deep, sensual harmony and a keen feeling of the "unity of human and animal life" that was acquired by Gauguin, if for a short time, far from France and European civilization.

Paul Gauguin. 1848–1903
Woman Holding a Fruit. *1893. Oil on canvas. 92 x 73 cm*

Pablo Picasso. 1881– 1973
Absinthe Drinker. 1901. *Oil on canvas. 73 x 54 cm*

On leaving the Post-Impressionists, we pass a long sequence of rooms featuring works by masters of the European avant-garde of the early twentieth century. The pride of place is occupied here by works of the two great twentieth-century artists — Picasso and Matisse. More than thirty paintings represent Picasso's restless youth — the dramatic works of the Blue and Pink Periods (until 1906) and the works of the Cubist Period (1907–14) — a trend created by Picasso and his friends. Following the lessons of Cézanne and other masters of Post-Impressionism, Picasso sought for the artistic idiom of his own, but he wanted to use this idiom for

Pablo Picasso. 1881– 1973. **Woman with a Fan (After the Ball).** *1908. Oil on canvas. 152 x 101 cm*

expressing universal and eternal values. With the help of the Cubist method he wanted to reveal the structural essence of objects and figures removing their trivial corporeal covering and laying bare the truth about the natural mechanism of human characters and living phenomena (*Woman with a Fan, La Fermière, Woman with a Mandolin*, etc.). In his works from the Late Cubist period he combined elements of diverse structures "synthesizing"

a new object, a new realm, such as the world of music, including instruments, sheets of music, wallpaper, etc.

In Matisse's art, eternal values express themselves through the language of colours. In his *Conversation*, the dusk of the blue unites by its dangerous tension the white-blue and black with the green in the male and female figures. The green and blue, symbols of the earth and the endless firmament, form a medium in which

Henri Matisse. 1869— 1954
Conversation. 1909. Oil on canvas. 177 x 217 cm

Henri Matisse. 1869—1954
The Dance. 1910. Oil on canvas. 270 x 391 cm

the fire of the red bodies creates the eternal Dance and the everlasting Music. Matisse created these famous panels in 1910 for Shchukin's mansion in Moscow. Nowadays one can see in the Hermitage thirty-seven canvases by Matisse from the period of his strenuous creative quests and the formation of his highly individual style. "My best works are preserved in Leningrad," said Matisse himself about them. Pervaded with love for the beauty of the world revealed in colour, they give birth to the atmosphere of musical harmony and pure spirituality.

An important addition to the panorama of French painting in the rooms of the Hermitage is sculpture — from the marbles by the great reformer Rodin, who embodied the eternal movement of life in the nearly impressionistically fluid and dynamic forms, to the bronzes of Matisse, Maillol and Bourdelle.

Auguste Rodin. 1840—1917
Eternal Spring. *1905. Marble. Height 77 cm*

Auguste Rodin. 1840—1917
Romeo and Juliet. *1905. Marble. Height 71 cm*

Wassily Kandinsky. 1866—1944
Composition No 6. *1913. Oil on canvas. 194 x 294 cm*

Five paintings represent the work of Wassily Kandinsky, the "father of modern Abstract Art", The widely known *Composition No 6* is a part of the series of early abstract canvases created by Kandinsky in 1911—12 in Germany during the period when the ideas of Abstract Art were in the process of "maturing". The composition is built on the combination of free colour spots devoid of any objective subject matter, on chromatic patches involved in a powerful movement dominated by elaborate, concerted rhythms. The painted surface "resounds" as a powerful chorus or symphonic music endowed with force, grandeur and jubilance. The start to geometric abstraction in twentieth-century art was given by the famous *Black Square* created by Casimir Malevich in 1915. In 2002 the Hermitage acquired

Wassily Kandinsky. 1866—1944
Winter. *1909. Oil on canvas. 70 x 97 cm*

a replica of this painting. The square of dense black colour, a symbol of the absence of light and hence of all colours of the world, applied on to the blinding white background, a symbol of light that took in all colours of the world, continues to excite us today, in the early twenty-first century, by its unresolved mystery. The painting by Malevich completes the tour of the rooms of nineteenth- and twentieth-century art.

Casimir Malevich. 1878— 1935. **Black Square** *1929— 30 (?). Oil on canvas. 53.5 x 53.5 cm*

On descending the staircase to the first floor we find ourselves in the rooms of the Winter Palace that once had served as the dwelling apartments of the imperial family. Today they house the exhibitions of the Department of the History of Russian Culture introducing visitors to various aspects of Russian culture from the six to twentieth century. Painting makes up only a part of the department's stocks and is represented mainly by

The Miracle of St George
and the Dragon. Late 15th — early 16th century
Tempera on panel. 57 x 43 x 2,5 cm

Dome of the Large Church of the Winter Palace

Alexei Antropov. 1716—95
Portrait of F. Dubiansky. 1761
Oil on canvas. 99.5 x 76.5 cm

traitists, however, still used the principles of icon-painting in their portraits for a long time. They endowed their models with a majestic immobility and an especial spiritual quality and embellished European clothes by Russian decorative patterns. Portraits are exhibited in the Russian department in a wide and varied context of objects of applied art. Furniture, tapestries, silver, porcelain, steelwork by celebrated Tula masters, carved ivory and costume — all that vividly re-creates the everyday life and atmosphere of various periods of Russian life.

Ivan Vishniakov. 1699—1761
Portrait of Stepanida Yakovleva
After 1756. Oil on canvas. 90 x 72 cm

a rich collection of ancient Russian icons and an interesting collection of portrait paintings. Many of these portraits, created by Russian and foreign painters active at the Russian court, had earlier been kept in the Winter Palace and other palaces of St Petersburg. Of especial artistic worth are early Russian portraits of the eighteenth century by such eminent artists as Matveyev, Nikitin, Antropov and Veshniakov. The art of portraiture came to Russia in the early eighteenth century together with Western European traditions, persistently inculcated by Peter the Great. Russian por-

The Malachite Drawing-Room
Objects in malachite

The pride of the Hermitage is the collection of Russian stone-carving art. Especially famous are articles made of malachite brought from the Urals. Tula masters have developed a special technique of malachite treatment. They skilfully sawed stones into thin plaques, pasted them to some surface prepared in advance and attained an amazing beauty of design and a wealth of shades of green. This so-called "Russian mosaic" technique was employed for the manufacture of the columns, fire-places and vases in the Malachite Drawing-Room of the Winter Palace. Nearly two tons of malachite presented to the Tsar by the owner of Urals plants Demidov went into the decoration of this interior. The Malachite Drawing-Room designed by Briullov after a devastating fire of 1837, the Malachite Drawing-Room is a part of the former Large Imperial Section of the Winter Palace.

The Malachite Drawing-Room. 1837—39
Architect: Vasily Briullov

The Library of Nicholas II. 1894
Architect: Alexander Krasovsky

The last inhabitants of the Large Imperial Section were Emperor Nicholas II and his family. The Small Dining-Room, intended for the family's meals, has retained its original decoration designed in the Rococo style by the architect Alexander Krasovsky in 1894. The historical appearance has also survived in the Library of Nicholas II. Its walls were upholstered with stamped leather and supplied with built-in carved furniture in the English Gothic style. After the fall of the monarchy, from July to October 1917, it was occupied by the Provisional Government. The Library was used as the reception room of Prime-Minister Kerensky. The Malachite Drawing-Room was the venue for the session of the government. It was here that the ministers assembled for the last time on 25 October and by the night of 26 October 1917 they were arrested in the neighbouring Small Dining-Room.

The Small Dining-Room. 1894
Architect: Alexander Krasovsky

The Concert Hall. 1837—39. Architect: Vasily Stasov

From the Malachite Room we enter the sumptuous Neva enfilade. It includes three interiors: the Concert Hall, the Ballroom or the Nicholas Hall (there was a portrait of Nicholas I in this room) — the largest hall in the entire palace, 1102 square metres in area, and the Anteroom on the side of the Main Staircase. The enfilade was designed by Vasily Stasov after the fire of 1837. It served as the venue for festive ceremonies, balls and festive dinners. Today the hall is used for large exhibitions. The Concert Hall preserves the tomb of the thirteen-century Russian army commander Prince St Alexander Nevsky. Peter the Great moved his holy relics to the Alexander Nevsky Monastery in St Petersburg at the beginning of the eighteenth century. The sarcophagus with the scenes of St Alexander Nevsky's victories is set against a pyramid framed with pediments bearing arms and standard lamps. About a ton and a half silver went into the production of the tomb.

The St Nicholas Hall. 1791–93; 1837–39
Architects: Giacomo Quarenghi; Vasily Stasov

Festive Dinner in the Concert Hall of the Winter Palace
in Honour of a Visit of the German Emperor William I in 1873. 1873
Watercolour by Mihaly Zichy

Display of the Department of Archaeology
5th—4th centuries B.C. Altai Mountains, Southern Siberia

Pile carpet. Detail. 5th—16th centuries B.C.
Altai Mountains, Southern Siberia
5th Pazyryk Barrow. Wool. 200 x 185 cm

On descending to the ground floor of the Winter Palace we find ourselves at the exhibition of the Department of Archaeology. We can see here monuments of the oldest cultures found by archaeologists in the territory of our country. World-famous are the finds from the barrows of Southern Siberia — the burial vaults of the chieftains of ancient nomads of the Altai Mountains. Thanks to the permafrost conditions the Altai barrows have reserved unique objects: decorations in the beast style of wood, leather and felt, Chinese silk, an immense felt carpet with coloured appliqué work, a wooden chariot and the world-earliest Oriental pile carpet.

Chariot. Wood. 5th—6th centuries B.C. Altai Mountains, Southern Siberia. 5th Pazyryk Barrow Wood, leather. Height 300 cm

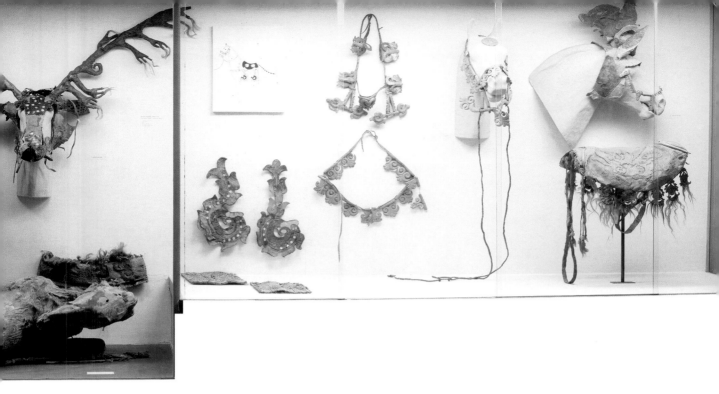

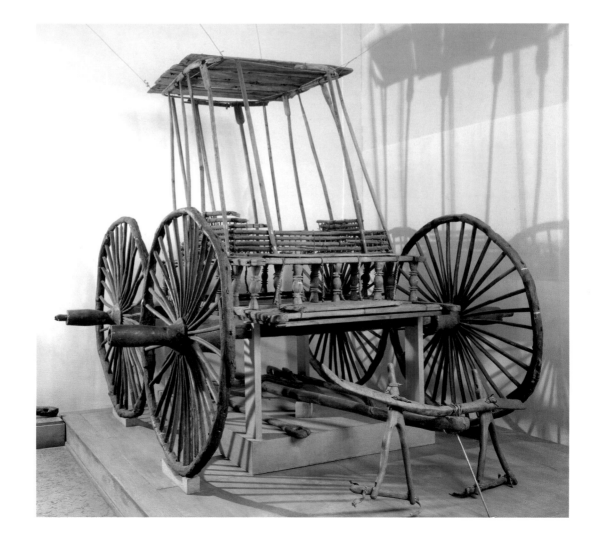

Diadem. 1st century A.D. Northern Black Sea Coast
Novocherkassk. The Khokhlach Barrow. Gold, turquoise, corals,
garnets, amethyst, glass, pearls. Length of circle 61 cm, height 15 cm

Next to the exhibition of the Department of Archaeology is a special repository known as the Gold Room of the Hermitage. It is here that the celebrated collections of Graeco-Scythian and Sarmatian gold and jewellery of the East can be seen. The Scythians, warlike nomadic tribes inhabiting the steppes adjoining the Black Sea Coast during the period from the seventh to the third century B.C., had contacts with the high civilization of the Ancient Greeks, who founded their cities-colonies in the Crimea in the sixth century B.C. This factor exerted a significant influence upon the specific features of the ancient jewellery, the wonderful examples of which began to be discovered in Scythian barrows and Greek burial vaults a long time ago. The golden comb from the Solokha Barrow on the

Comb. 4th century B.C. The Solokha Barrow
Gold. Height 12.3 cm, width 10.2 cm

Vessel depicting Scythians. 4th century B.C. Kerch
The Kul-Oba Barrow. Electrum. Height 13 cm

Dnieper (excavated in 1912—13) and a vessel of electrum (an alloy of gold and silver) from the Kul-Oba Barrow excavated in 1837 near Kerch were executed by the skilful hand of a Greek craftsman. Moreover, the articles were decorated with representations of Scythian warriors with realism and consummate mastery characteristic of the Greeks. A veritable masterpiece of the jewellery microtechnique are the famous Theodosia ear-rings dating from the fourth century B.C. Between the ear-ring disc and lunula is located a chariot with four harnessed horses driven by Nike, the goddess of Victory, and next to her is a warrior holding a shield. The lunula is covered with granulation and it can be seen only under a magnifying

Stag. 7th—6th centuries B.C. Northern Caucasus
The barrow near the Kostromskaya Station. Gold. Length 31.7 cm

Ear-ring. 4th century B.C. Greece. The Theodosia Barrow
Cast, chased and engraved gold, microtechnique. Height 9 cm

Jug. 10th—11th century, Egypt; 17th century, Turkey (decor)
Carved rock crystal, silver. Height 19.8 cm

*Table. 17th century. By Master Situram. India
Gold, diamonds, rubies, emeralds, pearls,
enamels. 27.3 x 27.3 cm*

glass that each grain consists of four drops. Unlike the Greeks, the Scythians depicted only beasts endowing them with magic power. The golden plaques in the form of stags and panthers are the rarest masterpieces of the Scythian "beast style". Graeco-Scythian traditions can be also traced in the barbaric art of the Sarmatians — the nomads who ousted the Scythians from the Black Sea Coast in the third century. The last displays of the Gold Room represent the jewellery items of the East: China, Egypt and India. Worthy of particular interest are precious objects of gold, gems and enamels — the gifts of Nadir-shah, the ruler of India, to the Russian Empress Anna Ioannovna.

*Jug. 17th century. India. Gold, diamonds,
rubies, emeralds. Height 26 cm*

Statue of the Pharaoh Amenemkhet III
Ca 1850–1800 B.C. Egypt. Granite. Height 86.5 cm

Before leaving the Winter Palace to continue a tour in the halls and rooms of other buildings of the Hermitage, let us pass the display of Ancient Egyptian art. Here we meet massive granite sarcophagi with carved inscriptions — hieroglyphs, monumental statues representing gods and rulers, filled with numerous wooden and bronze statuettes — *ushabti* depicting servants accompanying a nobly Egyptian to the netherworld. The great art of Ancient Egypt celebrated the might of the Pharaohs and served to express the Egyptians' belief in the life after death.

Stela representing the royal scribe Ili
Early 14th century B.C. Egypt
The New Kingdom. Limestone. 95 x 71 cm

Statuette of a man. Late 15th century B.C. Egypt
The New Kingdom. Wood. Height 34.5 cm

Room of Anciet Egyptian Culture and Art
5th thousand B.C. — late 1st thousand B.C.

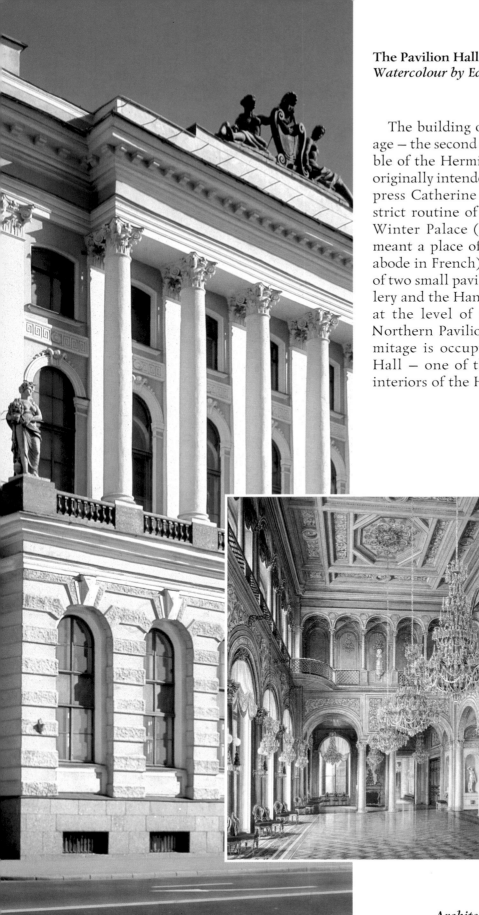

The Pavilion Hall. *1863*
Watercolour by Eduard Hau

The building of the Small Hermitage — the second edifice in the ensemble of the Hermitage complex — was originally intended for a repose of Empress Catherine the Great from the strict routine of life reigning in the Winter Palace (the word *hermitage* meant a place of solitude, a hermit's abode in French). The palace consists of two small pavilions linked by a gallery and the Hanging Garden located at the level of the first floor. The Northern Pavilion of the Small Hermitage is occupied by the Pavilion Hall — one of the most sumptuous interiors of the Hermitage.

The Pavilion Hall. 1850s
Architect: Andrei Stakenschneider. Detail

The Peacock Clock is the most spectacular exhibit of the Pavilion Hall. The clock was bought by Grigory Potemkin in 1788 in England. It was created by the outstanding English clock-maker James Cox and belong to the category of winding mechanisms fashionable in the eighteenth century and striking the public's imagination now as well. In a definite time the characters of the clock get "alive": the cock is crowing and flapping its wings, the owl turns its head and the peacock unfolds his beautiful tail. In the cap of the mushroom are moving the figures showing hours, minutes and seconds...

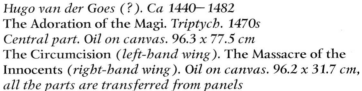

Hugo van der Goes (?). Ca 1440–1482
The Adoration of the Magi. Triptych. 1470s
Central part. Oil on canvas. 96.3 x 77.5 cm
The Circumcision (left-hand wing). The Massacre of the
Innocents (right-hand wing). Oil on canvas. 96.2 x 31.7 cm,
all the parts are transferred from panels

Reliquary-casket with scenes from the life
of St Valeria. Late 12th century. Limoges, France
Copper, champlevé enamels, wood
Height 19.5 cm, length 27.7 cm, width 11.7 cm

The two galleries of the Small Hermitage house well-known collections — of Western European medieval applied art and Netherlandish art of the fifteenth and sixteenth centuries. Among masterpieces of Netherlandish art is the triptych *Adoration of the Magi* by Hugo van der Goes. The three wings of this work feature episodes connected with the legend of the birth and childhood of Christ; in the background of the left wing shows the meeting of Mary and Elizabeth that had preceded the birth of Christ. The central panel deals with *The Adoration of the Magi*, while the right-hand wing depicts *The Massacre of the Innocents.*

Rogier van der Weyden is represented in the Hermitage by a large-scale painting, *St Luke Painting the Virgin*. Its subject is based on a Gospel story telling how the Evangelist St Luke painted a portrait of the Madonna and the Child after they had appeared to him.

Lucas van Leyden. 1489/94– 1533
The Healing of the Blind Man of Jericho. 1531
Triptych. Oil on canvas, transferred from a panel
115.5 x 150.5 cm (central part);
89 x 33.5 cm (side wings)

The well-known sixteenth-century Netherlandish master Lucas van Leyden is represented in the Hermitage by one of his best works — the triptych *The Healing of the Blind Man of Jericho*. This is the artist's only work in the Hermitage. The triptych has little in common with the religious compositions of the previous period. It has neither a profound prayer mood, nor a serious solemnity. The subject of Christ's healing of the blind man is treated by the artist as a motley genre scene filled with everyday

details. Probably the secular charac-
ter of the scene was due to the fact that
the painting was intended not for the
chancel of a cathedral, but for the Leyden Hospital, and the Gospel subject
played here a moral, edifying rather
than religious role. In the side wings
of the triptych, the artist placed, in-
stead of traditional representations of
saints, purely secular figures of a warrior and a maiden as heralds demonstrating the coat of arms of the com-
missioners — the Leyden burgher
Jacob Floriszon and his wife.

The Old Hermitage. 1771—87
Architect: Yuri Velten

The austere façade of the Large Hermitage (after the construction of the New Hermitage it began to be called the Old Hermitage) on the side of the Palace Embankment is a part of the architectural ensemble including the Small Hermitage and the Winter Palace. The interiors of the Small and Old Hermitage with their windows overlooking the Neva are divided by the Council Staircase (in the nineteenth century members of the State Council used it to get to the first floor). Today the rooms and halls of the Old Hermitage house a famous collection of Italian art of the Renaissance.

The Council Staircase
Architect: Andrei Stakenschneider

Simone Martini. Ca 1284—1344
The Madonna from The Annunciation scene
Ca 1340—44. Tempera on panel. 30.5 x 21.5 cm

The exhibition of Italian art occupies twenty-nine rooms and represents fully enough the great history of the Italian school of painting — from the Middle Ages to the eighteenth century. In the so-called Room of Italian Primitifs opening the collection there is a unique masterpiece by Simone Martini — the right-hand wing of a diptych, *The Annunciation*, representing *The Madonna*. The left-hand part of the diptych featuring *Archangel Gabriel* is now in the National Gallery in Washington.

Filippino Lippi. Ca 1457—1504
The Adoration of the Infant Christ
Mid-1480s. Oil on copper plate, transferred from a panel. Diameter 53 cm

Fra Beato Angelico da Fiesole. Ca 1400– 1455
Madonna and Child with Angels. *Ca 1425*
Tempera on panel . 80 x 51 cm

Leonardo da Vinci. 1452—1519. The Madonna and Child
(the Litta Madonna). *Ca 1490—91. Tempera on canvas,*
transferred from a panel. 42 x 33 cm

The two paintings by Leonardo da Vinci, a titan of the Renaissance, belong to the invaluable treasures of the Hermitage Museum. *The Litta Madonna* is executed in the medium of tempera traditional for Italian art. The image of the Madonna, in which physical perfection combines with spiritual elevation, is an ideal of High Renaissance beauty.

The Leonardo da Vinci Room. 1858—60
Architect: Andrei Stakenschneider

The largest cultural centres of the Italian Renaissance were located in cities, each of which was an independent political structure. Venice, along with Florence and Rome, made an immense contribution to the history of Italian painting. The flowering of Renaissance art in the most beautiful Italian city called a "gem of the Adriatic", was connected in the late fifteenth century with the name of the great Giorgione (Giorgio da Castelfranco). Giorgione lived but a short life — he was about thirty-two when he became a victim of plaque. Only about a dozen of Giorgione's indubitable works have reached us. Judith ranks with masterpieces of the Hermitage collection. Its subject is connected with a Biblical story about the Jewish beauty Judith, who penetrated into the camp of the Assyrian army that besieged her native town. Having charmed the army commander Holophernes by her beauty, she decapitated him and thus saved her compatriots from death. The heroic theme was very popular in the age of the Renaissance because it gave the artist an opportunity to depict his heroes as ideally beautiful. Judith with a sword in her hand trampling the head of the enemy, looks like a perfect ancient statue that is not aware of horrors of human being.

Giorgione (Giorgio da Castelfranco)
Ca 1478—1510. Judith. Early 1500s
Oil on canvas, transferred from
a panel. 144 x 66.5 cm

Titian (Tiziano Vecellio). 1485/90–1576
Repentant Mary Magdalene. 1560s
Oil on canvas. 119 x 97 cm

Significant works by major representatives of the Late Renaissance, Titian's followers, such as Jacopo Tintoretto, Paolo Veronese and Jacopo Palma el Vecchio, also testify to the flowering of the Venetian school.

The Lamentation was created by Paolo Veronese for the Venetian Church of San Giovanni e Paolo. In the seventeenth century the original work was sold to a private gallery and its place in the church was occupied by a copy. Veronese's painting — usually vivid, succulent, full of dynamism and abundance of characters — looks extremely austere and concise. The figures of the Madonna and the young golden-haired Angel supporting the body of Christ are full of tragic yet restrained mourning.

The painting of Titian became the culmination of Venetian art in the age of the Renaissance. His *Repentant Mary Magdalene*, featuring the repentant adulteress in the moment of her passionate prayer, belongs to his indubitable masterpieces. However, her image lacks austere asceticism or religious ecstasy — on the contrary, Mary Magdalene is beautiful by her earthly, real beauty. The painter's brush renders the wealth of hues of her golden hair, the softness of her white skin, the living vibration of her thin fingers, her arms folded in a thrust of prayer. Several wide brushstrokes bring out from darkness a crystal vessel filled with precious ambrosia .

Paolo Veronese (Paolo Caliari). 1528–1588
The Lamentation. *Between 1576 and 1582*
Oil on canvas. 147 x 111.5 cm

Raphael (Rafaello Santi). 1483– 1520
The Holy Family (The Madonna with the Beardless
St Joseph). Ca 1506. Tempera on canvas, transferred from a panel. 72.5 x 56.5 cm

The two works by Raphael — together with wonderful examples of Renaissance majolica, furniture, tapestry and sculpture — can be found in the so-called Raphael Room. The walls of the small study, next to the Raphael Room, are adorned with a series of nine frescoes devoted to the goddess of love Venus and executed after Raphael's sketches by his pupils for the Palatine Villa in Rome.

Dish depicting St Cecilia
Between 1540 and 1545. Deruta, Italy
Majolica, painting over white
opaque tin glazing, lustre. Diameter 41 cm

The display of paintings of the Italian Renaissance continues in the rooms of the New Hermitage. Raphael, a great master of the Renaissance, is represented in the Hermitage by two pictures, *The Conestabile Madonna* and *The Madonna with the Beardless St Joseph*, dating from the early period of the creative career of this genius of painting. *The Holy Family* was painted by a young yet already well-known artist in Florence, soon after his arrival there from Perugia. The image of the Madonna created by Raphael embodies the ideal of female beauty; "a certain idea", in the words of the artist himself, made up of a large number of beautiful faces seen by the artist in real life. St Joseph, who was traditionally painted as an old bearded man, is depicted by Raphael like an image of the artist's contemporary.

*The Raphael Room
(Room of 16th-Century Italian Majolica)*

Raphael (Rafaello Santi). 1483—1520
The Conestabile Madonna. Ca 1503
Oil on canvas, transferred from a panel. 17.5 x 18 cm

The Conestabile Madonna is a small-scale masterpiece created by the young Raphael in his native Perugia. The artist depicted the tender, maidenly fragile Madonna with the Infant Christ on her lap against the background of a light, thoroughly modelled spring landscape. The painting was produced on a panel and once had formed a single whole with its frame, probably made after a drawing by Raphael.

However, a poor state of the wooden support made the Hermitage restorers transfer Raphael's priceless painting from wood on to canvas immediately after the painting had arrived from Italy in 1871.

In the study where the frescoes of the Raphael school are exhibited, is one more world-famous masterpiece, *Crouching Boy* — the only sculpture by Michelangelo in the Hermitage.

The Study or Room of Frescoes of the Raphael School
Architect: Leo von Klenze

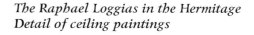

*The Raphael Loggias in the Hermitage
Detail of ceiling paintings*

One can form some idea about Raphael's mature period from the Hermitage's copy of the famous Raphael Loggias in the Vatican. Catherine the Great ordered the architect Giacomo Quarenghi to erect a building next to the Hermitage Theatre faithfully repeating the Vatican Gallery according to exact drawings. The copies of the Vatican frescoes, executed on canvas by the Roman painter Christoph Unterberger and his assistants, were set on the walls of the Loggias in St Petersburg in 1787—88.

*The Raphael Loggias. 1783—92
Architect: Giacomo Quarenghi*

In 1783 Empress Catherine the Great ordered her court architect Giacomo Quarenghi to build a new court theatre on the site of the decayed Winter Palace of Peter the Great, on the bank of the Winter Canal. The elegant Venetian arch spanning the Winter Canal united the white-stone building of the theatre and the façade of the Hermitage palaces into a single ensemble. The architect succeeded in creating a veritable architectural masterpiece that became one of the best palatial theatres of Europe. The architect used as the theatre's foundation the ground floor of the former Palace of Peter the Great and constructed over it a magnificent auditorium and a stage. The theatre begins with a vestibule located in the upper part of the arched bridge. The auditorium strikes one by its balanced and commensurate proportions. Taking the form of Roman theatres as a

The Hermitage Theatre. 1783—89. Architect: Giacomo Quarenghi

The Auditorium of the Hermitage Theatre

basis, Quarenghi arranged the rows of seats in the form of an amphitheatre. According to the architect's concept, "in this theatre any etiquette is discarded, there are no special seats and one can choose any place he or she likes." The theatre became the favourite place of Empress Catherine the Great. It perfectly combined all the best achievements of European theatrical architecture: beautiful acoustics, the stage suitable for any scenic activities, comfortable seats for viewers, with a sense of elegance and intimacy inherent to the domestic imperial theatre. The entire court, the heir's family and diplomats used to gather for performances, and sometimes there were up to 200 invited guests. The Empress watched the performances and not rarely wrote plays herself. The conductors of the theatre were European celebrities, such as Cimaroso, Galuppi and Paisiello. The companies of the best Russian and foreign actors and musicians performed at its stage.

The ground floor of the Hermitage Theatre houses a unique memorial display, "The Winter Palace of Peter the Great". In the course of the reconstruction of the theatre in 1987–89 were discovered surviving architectural fragments of the third, last Winter Palace of Peter the Great. Its construction had been started back in 1716 by Johann Mattarnovi and completed in 1723 by Domenico Trezzini. The re-created Dining-Room, Study and Turnery display an approximate set of objects from the Hermitage stocks, which were fashionable in the age of Peter the Great.

The posthumous "wax effigy" of the Tsar that can be now seen in the display of the Palace of Peter the Great was executed by the sculptor Carlo Bartolomeo Rastrelli on the orders of Catherine I. The figure was a faithful copy of the Emperor's outward appearance and stature made in wood, and only the hands, feet and face were of wax. All the things put on the figure of the Tsar who was very tall — 204 cm (6 feet 7 inches) — are authentic: the formal costume embroidered with silver, the Order of St Andrew the First-Called with a red order ribbon, shoes and even the wig made of Peter's hair.

Carlo Bartolomeo Rastrelli. 1675–1744
Wax effigy of Peter the Great. 1725. Wax, wood. Height 204 cm

The Winter Palace of Peter the Great. The Turnery

The main façade of the New Hermitage from Millionnaya Street. 1842—51. Architect: Leo von Klenze

The New Hermitage is the fifth building in the Hermitage complex. The idea to construct a special edifice for storing the Hermitage collections and for creating in it a museum open for the public at large belonged to Emperor Nicholas I. Such museums had already been established in Europe back at the beginning of the nineteenth century. The masterpieces of world culture preserved in the palatial and private collections were made accessible to the educated public after the end of the Napoleonic Wars, in the period of democratization of European society. By opening the first public museum in St Petersburg Russia joined the general course of European cultural policy. The design of the museum that would be later named the New Hermitage was commissioned from the Bavarian architect Leo von Klenze, who had already had an experience of constructing museum buildings. The main façade of the New Hermitage was directed southwards and overlooked Millionnaya Street. The Russian architects, Vasily Stasov and his assistant Nikolai Yefimov, supervised the construction of the museum. The official inauguration of the museum took place on 7 February 1852.

Portico of the New Hermitage with the granite statues of Atlantes. 1840s. Sculptor: Alexander Terebenev

The ornate staircase of the New Hermitage leads us to the halls and rooms of the first floor where the collection of Western European art is displayed. Decorative vases of semi-precious stones, manufactured at the Peterhof, Ekaterinburg and Kolyvan Factories, adorn the upper landing of the staircase. One can also see here a collection of marble statues acquired by Emperor Nicholas I in 1845 in Rome, during his visits to the studios of the then fashionable Neo-Classical masters, the Italians Lorenzo Bratolini, Giovanni Dupré and Luigi Bienaimé, as well as the Germans Emil Wolf, Rudolf von Schadow and others.

Scipione Tadolini. 1788– 1868
Ganymedes with an Eagle. 1845. *Marble*

Pietro Tenerani. 1798– 1869
Venus and Cupid Taking Out a Splinter from Her Foot. 1845. *Marble*

The rooms of the first floor of the New Hermitage open the Gallery of the History of Ancient Painting. According to Klenze's concept, it was to serve as a sort of introduction to the history of world art and a start of one's tour of European painting represented in the halls and rooms of the Picture Gallery. Legends about the unique mastery of ancient painters, whose works have not reached us, as well as subjects from ancient history were interpreted by the Munich artist Georg Hiltensperger in the series of paintings hung on the walls of the gallery. They were painted in the medium of encaustics, or wax paints on copper plates. In 1861 the collections of works by the two leading masters of Neo-Classicism of the late eighteenth and early nineteenth centuries, the Italian Antonio Canova and the Dane Berthel Thorvaldsen, whose first works had been purchased by Alexander I, began to be installed in the Gallery. The famous sculptural group *The Three Graces* commissioned from Canova by the French Empress Joséphine de Beauharnais, Napoleon's first wife, enjoyed particular renown.

Antonio Canova. 1757– 1822
The Three Graces. 1813 *Marble*
Height 182 cm

> *The Large Italian Skylighted Room*
Architect: Leo von Klenze

119

Antonio Canale (Canaletto). 1697—1768
Reception of the French Ambassador in Venice. 1726
Oil on canvas. 181 x 259.5 cm

The three main interiors on the first floor of the New Hermitage are known as "Skylighted Rooms". Light pours into them from above, through their glazed ceilings — top lighting was always thought to be most profitable for painting. The skylighted rooms were intended for large paintings — the vast spaces of the walls are covered with an even layer of a dark-red paint in imitation of cloth that had lined the walls originally. In the central hall — the Large Skylighted Room — are exhibited large-scale works of the Italian school of the seventeenth and eighteenth centuries. A true marvel of the collection is the picture *Reception of the French Ambassador in Venice* by the brilliant Venetian landscape painter Antonio Canaletto.

The painting *The Triumph of an Army Commander* by Giovanni Battista Tiepolo, a major Venetian painter of the eighteenth century, is part of the series of five-large-scale canvases created for the decoration of the Palazzo Dolfino in Venice. The artist portrayed here Manius Curtius Dandatus, a Roman army commander of the third century B.C., who won a victory over Pirrhus and captured elephants as his trophy.

Giovani Battista Tiepolo. 1696— 1770. **The Triumph of an Army Commander.** *Ca 1725. Oil on canvas. 546 x 322 cm*

Caravaggio (Michelangelo Merisi da Caravaggio). 1571– 1610
Lute Player. *Ca 1595. Oil on canvas. 94 x 119 cm*

Among numerous masterpieces of Italian art in the Hermitage there are paintings which serve as hallmarks of the supreme level of the collection. One of these is the famous *Lute Player* — the Hermitage's only work by the great Caravaggio.

The content of this painting has been interpreted in many research works, which offer various interpretations of its subject matter. The most popular one is an opinion that the subject of this work is related to the theme of *vanitas*, an idea of the imminent death of everything alive.

The flowering youth of the lute player is but a transient phase, as reminded by the broken string of the lute, by the flowers that would wither and by the fruit that would wrinkle and dry out. Another interpretation treats the painting as a symbolic representation of the five senses: the flowers allude to smell, the fruit to taste, the sheet of music to eyesight and the sound of music to hearing, while the especial ponderability, three-dimensional quality of all details in the picture allude to the possibility of their sensual perception.

Tintoretto (Jacopo Robusti). 1518– 1594
The Birth of St John the Baptist. *Ca 1550. Oil on canvas. 181 x 266 cm*

Luca Giordano. 1632– 1705. **The Battle of Lapiths and the Centaurs**
Late 17th century. Oil on canvas. 255 x 390 cm

El Greco (Domenico Theotokopoulos). 1541– 1614
The Apostles Peter and Paul. *Between 1587 and 1592*
Oil on canvas. 121.5 x 105 cm

Francisco de Zurbarán. 1598– 1664
The Girlhood of the Madonna. *Ca 1660*
Oil on canvas. 73.5 x 53.5 cm

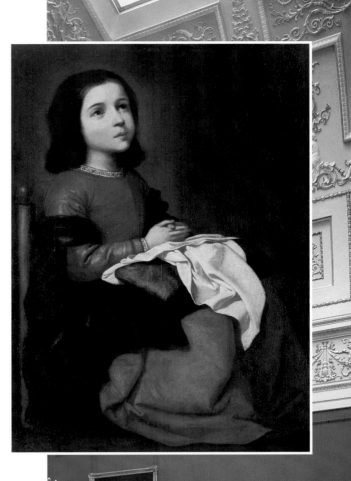

At the beginning of the nineteenth century the Hermitage had formed a comparatively small collection of painting — about 150 works, which might be regarded as a representative one in comparison with other museums of the world. The collection mainly represents the best achievements of the "Golden Age" of Spanish art — the seventeenth century. In the New Hermitage the paintings by the famous artists Velázquez, Murillo, Zurbarán and Ribera are displyaed in the so-called Large Spanish Skylighted Room. In the twentieth century the Hermitage collection of Spanish painting has been enriched with two masterpieces — in 1911 the famous canvas *The Apostles Peter and Paul* by El Greco was acquired, and in 1972, the portrait of the actress Antonia Zárate by Francisco de Goya.

Francisco de Goya. 1746– 1828. **Portrait of Antonia Zárate.** *Ca 1811. Oil on canvas. 71 x 58 cm*

The Hermitage collection of Dutch painting of the seventeenth century — the "Golden Age" of Dutch culture. This school is not represented anywhere else in the world beyond the borders of Holland with such fullness as in the Hermitage. The museum boasts a unique collection of Rembrandt Harmensz van Rijn, a painter of genius, whose works can be found in one of the large halls of the New Hermitage. More than twenty pictures represent a difficult creative path of the master in the course of the four centuries, from early works executed in a traditional elaborate manner that brought him a success to his later, profound and tragic canvases understood only by the artist's rare adherents. The monumental painting *The Return of the Prodigal Son* became an embodiment of the great master's philosophical thoughts about life.

The Rembrandt Room

Rembrandt Harmensz van Rijn. 1606— 1669
The Return of the Prodigal Son. *Ca 1668— 69*
Oil on canvas. 262 x 205 cm

Rembrandt Harmensz van Rijn. 1606— 1669
Danaë. 1636— 1642. Oil on canvas. 185 x 202.5 cm

The subject of *Danaë*, one of Rembrandt's most celebrated paintings, is based on an ancient Greek myth. Danaë, the only daughter of King Acrisius, was doomed for solitude in a tower. She was imprisoned there by her father, because a priestess prophesied that he would die from the hand of his own grandson. However, Zeus, the supreme god, attracted by the beauty of Danaë, penetrated to her bedroom in the form of a golden shower.

In 1985 a maniac poured sulphuric acid on to the picture and made two cuts with a knife in the canvas. The treasure seemed to have been lost forever. But the strenuous efforts of experienced Hermitage restorers that lasted for about twelve years allowed to bring the painting back to life.

Rembrandt Harmensz van Rijn. 1606—69. Flora. 1634
Oil on canvas. 125 x 101 cm

The Tent-Roof Hall
Architect: Leo von Klenze

The Tent-Roof Hall of the New Hermitage houses one of the richest collections of seventeenth-century Dutch art. A special feature of the collection is the combination of an immense quantity (more than a thousand paintings) with the abundance of masterpieces — practically all major painters of the "Golden Age" of Dutch culture are represented here. The culmination period in the history of Dutch painting was the middle of the seventeenth century. The majority of the masters (generally known as the "Small" Dutchmen) painted works on a small scale as commissions of local burghers, who preferred to adorn their homes with scenes of everyday life, portraits, still lifes and landscapes of their homeland. Each artist specialized in a special, clearly indicated scope of themes, contributing to a great variety of Dutch art. There were several artistic centres, in which well-known Dutch artists lived and worked — Amsterdam, Haarlem,

Utrecht, Delft, Leyden and The Hague. Pictures by the "Small" Dutchmen attracted not only by their subject matter, but also by their elaborate colour range, virtuoso rendering of air and light medium and textural variety of the objects portrayed, in which these painters were unrivalled in the seventeenth century.

Frans Hals, a great portraitist of the seventeenth century, is represented in the Hermitage by two fine examples of his painting. In his *Portrait of a Young Man Holding a Glove* the artist, working in a free manner not typical of

Frans Hals. Between 1581 and 1585— 1666
Portrait of a Young Man Holding a Glove
Ca 1650. Oil on canvas. 80 x 66.5 cm

Dutch painting, without a careful observation of details, captures the essence of a rapidly fleeting moment.

The Revellers is a masterpiece by Jan Steen, a brilliant painter of everyday scenes, the most attentive and witty Dutch artist. In the images of the intoxicated merrymakers the artist depicted himself and his wife Margaretha, the daughter of the landscape painter Jan van Goyen. As usual with Steen, this amusing incident conceals a moral message that an incorrect mode of living is fraught with ill after-effects.

Jan Steen. 1625/26— 1679. The Revellers
Ca 1660. Oil on panel. 39 x 30 cm

Pieter de Hooch. 1629 — after 1684
Mistress and Her Maid in a Courtyard
Ca 1660. Oil on canvas. 53 x 42 cm

The type of still life called "breakfast" was one of the most popular in Dutch painting. The overturned goblet, crumpled tablecloth and the knives and forks in disarray — all these features suggest the presence of a man, who seems to have just left the room. Willem Claesz Heda was the leading master of this genre. Objects in his paintings, the best of which might be considered *Breakfast with a Lobster*, is almost entirely devoid of bright saturated colours. But merging into an elegant restrained gamut, they create a strikingly beautiful chromatic chord.

Willem Claesz Heda. 1594 — between 1680 and 1682
Breakfast with a Lobster. 1648. Oil on canvas. 118 x 118 cm

Gerard Terborch. 1617— 1681. A Glass of Lemonade. 1660s
Oil on canvas, transferred from a panel. 67 x 54 cm

The Room of 17th-Century Flemish Painting (The Snyders Room)

The art of Flanders is represented in the Hermitage with a nearly exhaustive completeness. More than five hundred paintings in a variety of genres — multifigured compositions of allegorical and religious content, portraits, still lifes, landscapes and everyday scenes demonstrating the mastery of more than 140 painters, allow the museum to show all the specific features of the leading seventeenth-century schools of painting. The Hermitage owns large collections of the most significant Flemish masters — about forty works by Pieter Paul Rubens, the head of the Flemish school, twenty-four works by the famous portrait painter Anthonis van Dyck, monumental canvases by Frans Snyders, Jacob Jordaens and Paul de Voos, genre paintings by David Teniers and Adrian Brouwer.

Anthonis van Dyck. 1599—1641. Portrait of Sir Thomas Wharton
Second half of the 1630s. Oil on canvas. 217 x 128.5 cm

Anthonis van Dyck. 1599— 1641. Family Portrait (Portrait of the Landscape
Painter Jan Wildens?). *Late 1621. Oil on canvas. 113.5 x 93.5 cm*

David Teniers the Younger. 1610— 1690
Peasant Wedding. *1650. Oil on canvas. 82 x 108 cm*

Jacob Jordaens. 1593—1678
The Bean King. Ca 1638. Oil on canvas. 157 x 211 cm

Frans Snyders. 1579–1657. Fruit Shop
Between 1618 and 1621. Oil on canvas. 206 x 342 cm

Pieter Paul Rubens. 1577— 1640
Perseus and Andromeda. *Early 1620s. Oil on canvas. 99.5 x 139 cm*

The Hermitage collection allows one to fully appreciate the creative scope of the outstanding Flemish master Pieter Paul Rubens. It seems that every Hermitage painting by Rubens demonstrates new facets of his powerful gift. The artist's skill endows with living energy the most abstract, speculative motifs. *The Union of Earth and Water* is an allegory celebrating the union of the two elements, in which Earth is personified by Cybele, the nature goddess, and Water by the sea-god Neptune.

Perseus and Andromeda ranks with masterpieces of the collection. This canvas, that has not lost the freshness of its colours, illustrates the mythological subject about the feat of Perseus, the son of Zeus and Danaë. The hero slew a monster to whom the daughter of the Ethiopian King was sacrificed and released the captive girl, thus winning the beauty's love.

> *The Knights' Hall*

Pieter Paul Rubens. 1577— 1640
The Union of Earth and Water. *Ca 1618. Oil on canvas. 222.5 x 180.5 cm*

Просьба   Don't touch
экспонаты   the exhibit
не трогать   please

The Hall of Roman Decorative Sculpture of the
1st and 2nd Centuries A.D. (the Peristyle Courtyard)

The Hall of Venus of Tauride

The collection of art of Classical Antiquity is arranged in the specially designed large halls of the ground floor of the Hermitage. The walls lined with stucco, an artificial marble of noble shades, emphasizes the grand statues of white marble. The rows of slender painted vases, articles of glass and metal as well as gems naturally co-exist in the space created by the architect's talent. The balance of proportions inherent to Classical Antiquity marks also the museum equipment: pediments used for sculpture, showcases, cupboards and furniture intended for visitors are executed in the "neo-Greek" style according to drawings by Leo von Klenze. The classically austere design of the halls — the columns, caryatids under the vaults, the elegant Greek ornaments in the paintings of the floors and ceilings, the coloured marbles of the floors, all serves as a matching mount for the noble beauty of the art of the ancient world.

Venus of Tauride. Roman copy from a Greek original by a sculptor of the Praxiteles circle. 3rd century B. C. Marble. Height 169 cm

The space of the Hall of Twenty Columns that was designed specially for an exhibition of ancient painted vases looks like an ancient Greek temple. The two rows of granite columns support the beams of the ceiling divided into squares. In the upper part of the walls are twelve compositions representing designs of vase paintings unfolded, as it were, on the plane. The gem of the Hermitage ceramic collection is the luxurious hydria, the veritable "Queen of Vases" that was discovered during the excavations of an ancient necropolis. The shoulders of the vase bear relief depictions of the rituals devoted to the cult of Demeter, the goddess of the earth and fecundity. The body of the vase is coated with black lacquer and it is skirted with a skilfully moulded relief shaped as griffins and lions. The room also houses a small but valuable collection of Etruscan bronzes.

Hydria with a scene of Eleusine mysteries (the "Queen of Vases"). 4th century B.C. Cumae, Campania. Earthenware, reliefs, painted decoration. Height 62.2 cm

The Hall of Twenty Columns

Funerary urn. Mid-4th century. Etruria. Bronze
Height 42 cm; length of the pediment 69 cm

Statue of Jupiter. 1st century A.D. Rome
Marble, tinted plaster. Height 347 cm

A very valuable part of the Hermitage collection of Classical Antiquity is a collection of Roman portraits. The best examples of this collection are displayed in the hall originally intended for Western European sculpture. For this reason Leo von Klenze adorned the vault of this hall with low-relief portraits of major European and Russian sculptors — Michelangelo, Thorvaldsen, Canova, Martos and Rauch.

In the centre of the hall stands a monumental statue of Jupiter, the supreme god of the Romans that was modelled on the extinct masterpiece of the great sculptor Phidias active in the fifth century B.C. The ancient Greek master created the statue of Zeus in the chryselepnatine technique or the

Bust of Empress Salonina
Mid-3rd century. Marble. Height 57 cm

Portrait of the Roman Emperor Philip I the Arab
3rd century. Rome. Marble. Height 70 cm

combination of ebony and gold. The Hermitage statue once had been produced by the acrolithic method, which combined marble for the extremities and gilded wood for the rest of the figure. The lost wooden details have been replaced by tinted plaster.

One of the most remarkable portraits of the third and second centuries represented in the room is the portrait of the "soldier" Emperor Philip I the Arab, a veritable masterpiece of the Hermitage collection. The likeness of Julia Cornelia Salonina, the spouse of Emperor Gallenus, is designed in the best traditions of Roman portrait sculpture of the third century. Â.C.

The Kolyvan Vase. 1847. The Kolyvan Lapidary Works, Altai Mountains
Revniukha jasper. Height 2.5 m, diameter 4.5 m

The famous Kolyvan vase, made of Revniukha jasper, is a fine example of Russian stone-carving. It has found its place in a room on the ground floor of the New Hermitage just by chance. Like other numerous vases of coloured semi-precious stone it was created specially for decorating the rooms of the first floor, but weighing too much — some nineteen tons — proved to be too heavy for the intended place above.

The vase is made up of five collapsible monolithic blocks; the diameter of the vase made of a single block of jasper is about five metres. The craftsmen of the Kolyvan Lapidary Works in the Altai Mountains worked on making the large vase for twelve years using as a model examples of ancient ceramics. That is why this monumental structure does not look alien among works by ancient artists.

One of the Hermitage's most famous masterpieces of ancient glyptics, the celebrated Gonzaga Cameo is a rare example of large "dynastic" carved stones. It features the rulers of Egypt Ptolemy II Philadelphus and his wife Arsinoë. The three-layer sardonyx of rare beauty of which the cameo is made, enabled the carvers to stress colour effects — the lower dark layer serves as a background against which the lighter matt profiles are clearly seen and the brownish upper layer is used to convey the hair, helmet and clothes. The cameo was presented by Joséphine de Beauharnais,

Cameo: Ptolemy II and Arsinoë II. (The Gonzaga cameo). 3rd century B.C. Alexandria Sardonyx. 15.7 x 11.8 cm

Napoleon's first wife, to Emperor Alexander I. No less famous is another Hermitage masterpiece — the pelike *The First Swallow* — a red-figure-vessel for wine decorated with a fine painted design. The man, youth and boy are shown looking at a swallow flying over their heads. The inscriptions allow us to reproduce their conversation: "Look, there is a swallow," says the man. "Yes, it is a swallow indeed, I swear by Hercules," exclaims the youth. "Here it is! Spring has come," rejoices the boy.

Red-figure pelike: The First Swallow
Ca 510 B.C. Attica, the Workshop of Euphronios
Earthenware, painted decoration. Height 37.5 cm

Reliquary in the form of deacon (St Etienne) Late 12th century. France. Silver-gilt, wood, gems, semi-precious stones. Height 42.5 cm

Processional cross of St Trudpert (known as the Freiburg Cross). Second half of the 13th century Silver, gold, gems, semi-precious stones, cloisonné enamel, gilding. Height 71.5 cm

The rooms of the ground floor of the New Hermitage include a special display that can be seen only in the company of a special guide. This is the so-called Brilliant Room — a collection of jewellery, gold and silver objects. The collection of jewellery began to take shape in the Hermitage during the reign of Empress Catherine the Great. One room in her apartments was allotted for the preservation of valuable objects and royal regalia and was known as the Brilliant Apartment. The present-day Brilliant Room also preserves unique golden articles from ancient barrows and the most precious examples of Western European art. The items of jewellery of the Russian Imperial Court include

Bouquet of flowers of gems and semi-precious stones in golden and silver mounts 1740s St Petersburg, by Jérémie Posier (?) Gold, silver, brilliants, gems, semi-precious stones, glass, fabric. 13 x 19 cm

a unique copy (reduced ten times) of the royal regalia produced for Empress Catherine the Great by her court master Jérémie Posier. The regalia consist of the large crown, the sceptre, the orb and the small crown made later for the consort of Emperor Alexander I and now kept in the Diamond Fund in Moscow. The copy was created by the celebrated jeweller Carl Fabergé specially for the Paris World Fair of 1900 and won there the Grand-Prix and the Large Gold Medal. The master himself was bestowed with the title of the best jeweller of Europe.

The General Staff building (1818—27)
Architect: Carlo Rossi. View from Palace Square

The powerful five-hundred-metre arc of the General Staff building skirting Palace Square from the south, forms together with the Winter Palace one of the most beautiful ensembles of St Petersburg. The two wings of this magnificent monument of Russian architecture dating from the age of Classicism are linked by a triumphal arch crowned with the Chariot of Glory. The left wing of the edifice — running from the triumphal arch to the Moika Embankment — was transferred to the Hermitage in the 1990s. The building had no major repair in the years of Soviet power and so it urgently needed serious reconstruction. Despite all difficulties, however, some of the halls have already been opened after restoration to become a new functioning part of the present-day Hermitage complex. Besides the new exhibitions "Beneath the Sign of the Eagle: Art of the Empire" and "Pierre Bonnard and Maurice Denis: Decorative Ensembles in the Hermitage Collection", which enabled visitors to see the works previously kept in the reserves due to a lack of display rooms in the Hermitage, the new premises are also used for temporary exhibitions, primarily those devoted to twentieth-century art. The new rooms are now also employed for the dem-

Objects from the Egyptian Service. 1806—08
Painted decoration after drawings by Dominique Vivant Denon
Sèvres Porcelain Factory, France. Porcelain, painted over a glaze and gilded

The General Staff building. The Ballroom. 1819—27
Living apartments of Karl Nesselrode. Architect: Carlo Rossi

The General Staff building. The Dining-Room. 1819—27
Living apartments of Karl Nesselrode. Architect: Carlo Rossi

onstration of present-day, more radical phenomena in contemporary world art. Thus, the Hermitage becomes a centre of both classical and modern culture.

The Hermitage wing of the General Staff building had been originally erected for the Ministry of Finance and Foreign Affairs. The formal, first floor of the building was occupied by the Minister of Foreign Affairs (the State Chancellor). The first owner of these apartments was Count Karl Nesselrode (1780—1862). The design of the apartments, created by Carlo Rossi at the beginning of the nineteenth century, happily survived from the time of Nesselrode almost intact. Here, in the authentic Empire-style interiors are now exhibited examples of applied art from this period demonstrating the brilliant workmanship of Russian and French artists in the age of Alexander I and Napoleon.

View of Palace Square and the building of the Winter Palace
from the Arch of the General Staff building

Эрмитаж

Путешествие по залам (на английском языке)

Издательство «Альфа-Колор», Санкт-Петербург
Тел./ФАКС (812) 326-8384 E-MAIL: alfac@mail.wplus.net